New Classics to Moderns

5

Contents

Yorktown Music Press

2-Part Invention No.12 in A Major

BWV 783

Johann Sebastian Bach
1685–1750

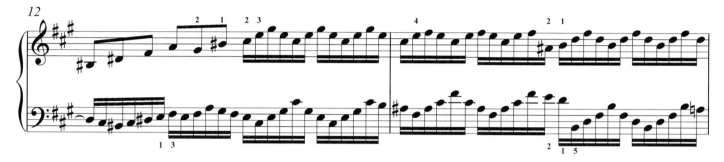

Fantasia in B Minor

Georg Philipp Telemann
1681–1767

Allegro

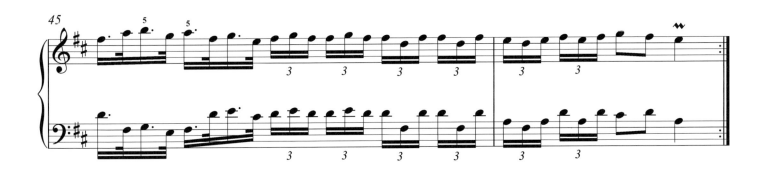

Con pompa

D.C. al Fine

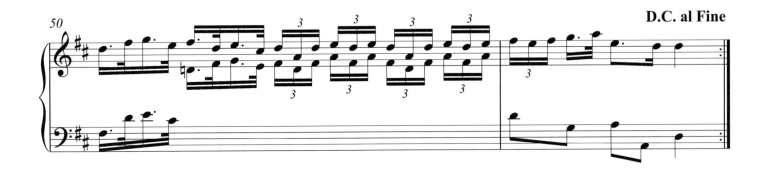

Allegro

from Sonata in A Major

Giovanni Battista Pergolesi
1710–1736

Allegro

Andante Di Molto

from Sonata Op. 5, No. 2

Johann Christian Bach
1735–1782

Andante di molto

Rondo

from Piano Sonata in C Major, K.545

Wolfgang Amadeus Mozart
1756–1791

RONDO
Allegro

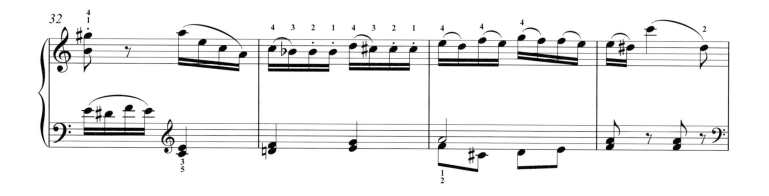

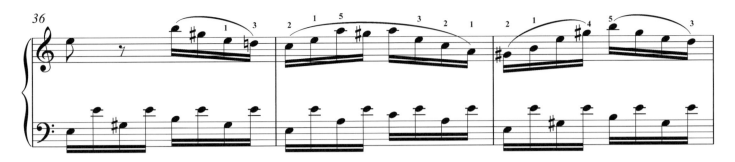

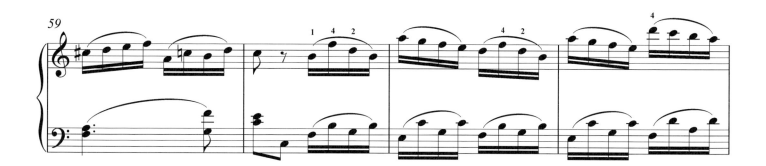

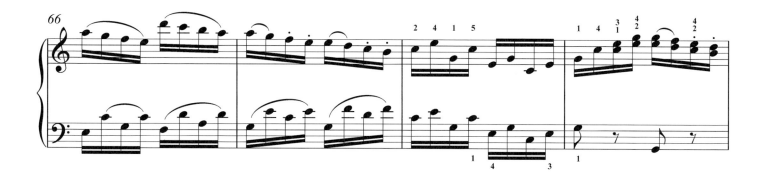

Chanson Populaire

from Album For The Young

Peter Ilyich Tchaikovsky
1840–1893

Prélude No.10

from Préludes (Book II)

Claude Debussy
1862–1918

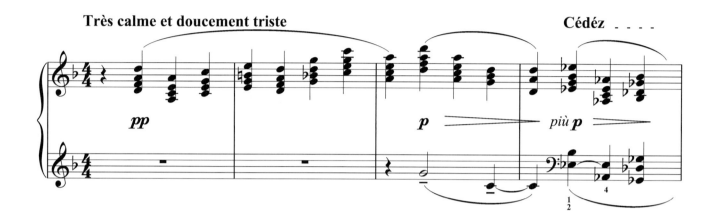

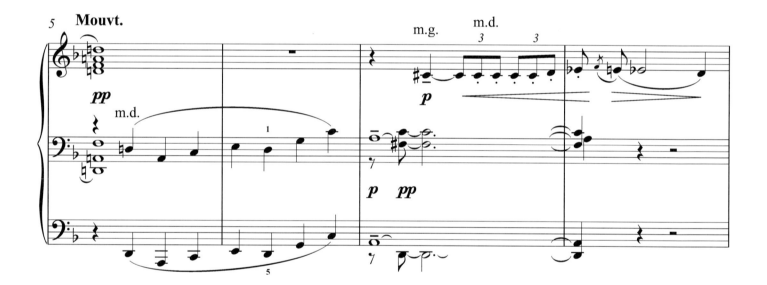

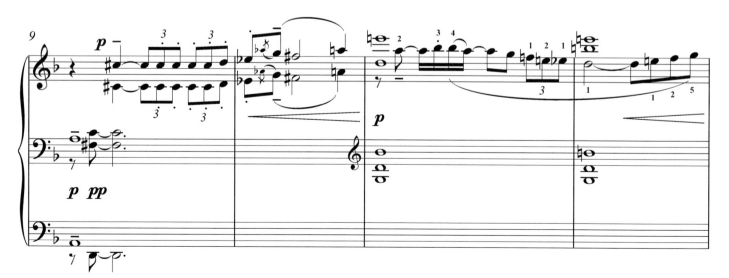

Animez un peu

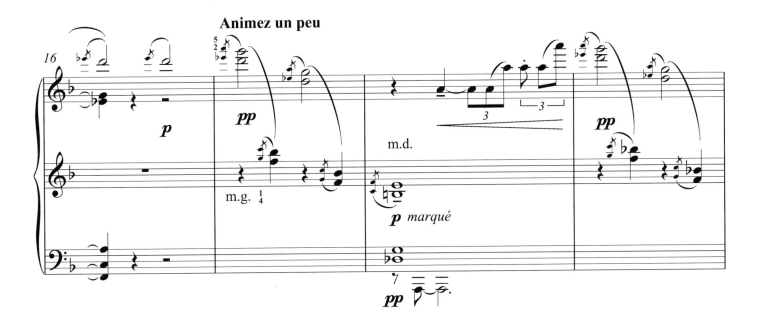

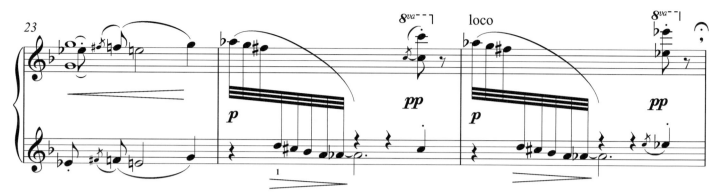

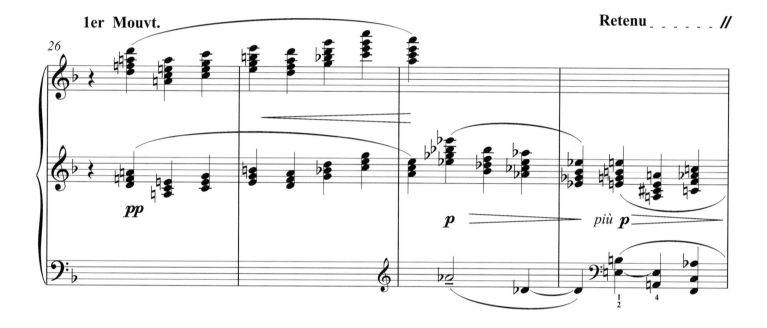

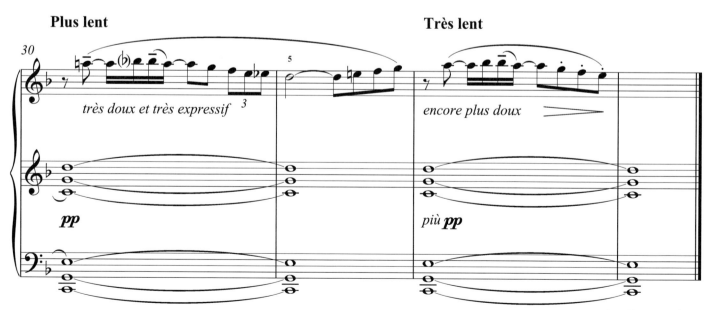

(...Canope)

Pavane Of The Sleeping Beauty

from Mother Goose

Maurice Ravel
1875–1937

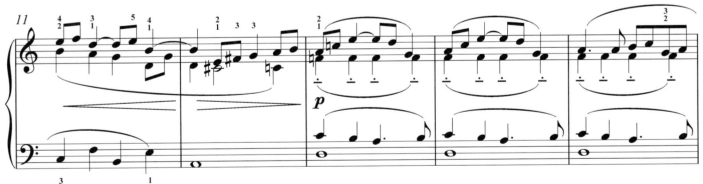

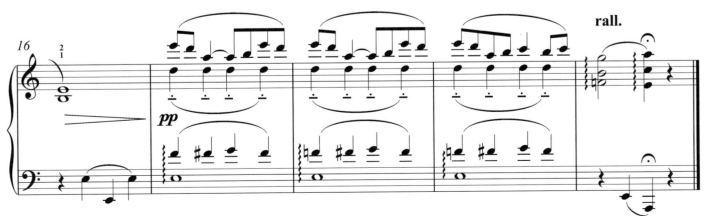

Allegro

No.2 *from* Les Cinq Doigts

Igor Stravinsky
1882–1971

A cheval

No. 3 *from* Promenades

Francis Poulenc
1899–1963

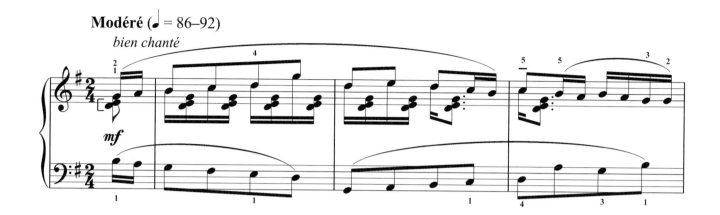

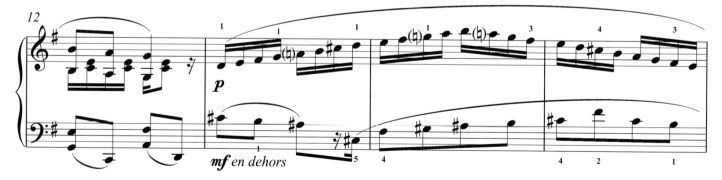

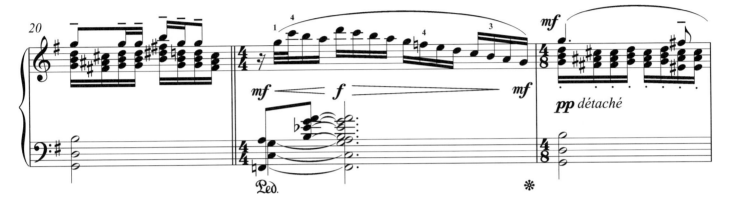

Bagatela No.8

from Once Bagatelas

Rodolfo Halffter
1900–1987

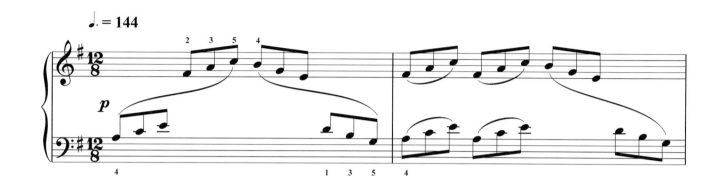

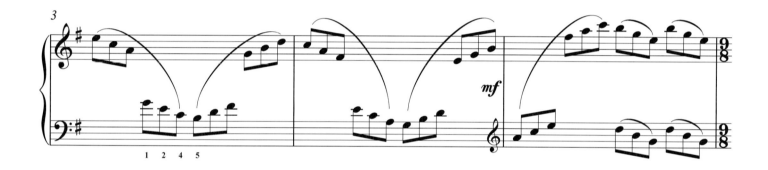

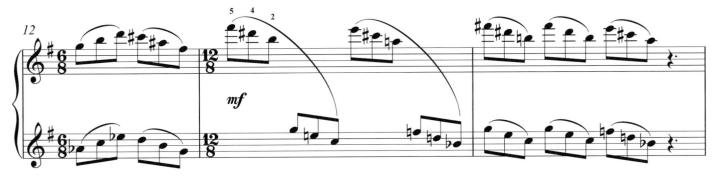

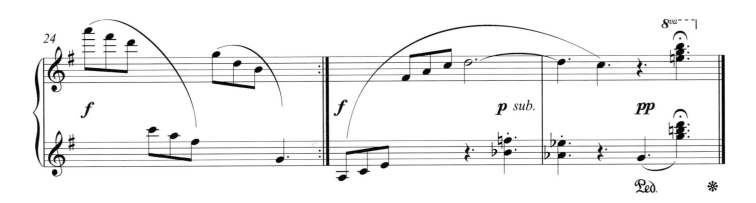

The Grove

from Folk Melodies

Witold Lutoslawski
1913–1994

Allegro vivace ♩ = *c*.88

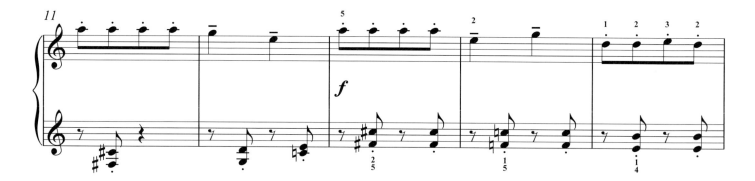

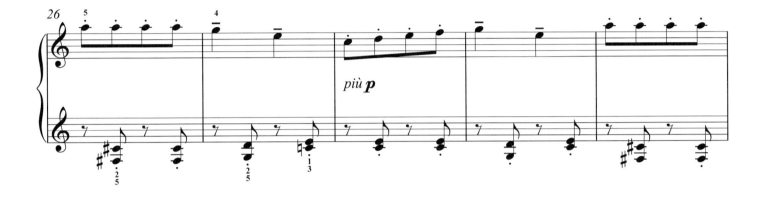

c. 30"

Trembling Leaves

Stanley Glasser
b.1926

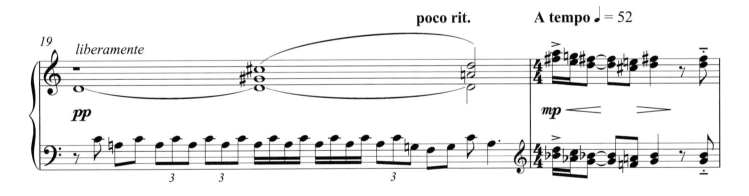

Exclusive Distributors:
Hal Leonard
7777 West Bluemound Road,
Milwaukee, WI 53213
Email: info@halleonard.com

Hal Leonard Europe Limited
42 Wigmore Street, Marylebone,
London WIU 2 RY
Email: info@halleonardeurope.com

Hal Leonard Australia Pty. Ltd.
4 Lentara Court, Cheltenham,
Victoria 9132, Australia
Email: info@halleonard.com.au

Order No. YK22154
ISBN 978-1-78305-375-9

Edited by Sam Lung.
Music processing and layout by Camden Music Services.

Printed in the EU.

www.halleonard.com